What Can Fly?

Patricia Whitehouse

Heinemann Library
Chicago, Illinois

© 2004 Heinemann Library
a division of Reed Elsevier Inc.
Chicago, Illinois

Customer Service 888-454-2279
Visit our website at www.heinemannlibrary.com

Designed by Sue Emerson, Heinemann Library; Page layout by Que-Net Media™
Printed and bound in the U.S.A. by Lake Book Manufacturing
Photo research by Bill Broyles

08 07 06 05 04
10 9 8 7 6 5 4 3 2 1

Library of Congress Cataloging-in-Publication Data
Whitehouse, Patricia, 1958-
  What can fly? / Patricia Whitehouse.
      v. cm. – (What can?)
Contents: What is flying? – How do living and nonliving things fly? – Can birds fly? – Can bugs fly? – How many wings do things need? – Can fish fly? – Can people fly?
  ISBN 1-4034-4365-3 (HC), 1-4034-4372-6 (Pbk.)
 1. Flight–Juvenile literature. 2. Animal flight–Juvenile literature. [1. Flight. 2. Animal flight.] I. Title.
  QP310.F5W48 2003
  573.7'98–dc21

                                    2003001020

Acknowledgments
The author and publishers are grateful to the following for permission to reproduce copyright material:
p. 4 M. C. Chamberlain/DRK Photo; p. 5 George J. Sanker/DRK Photo; p. 6 Maslowski/Visuals Unlimited; p. 7 Chris Collins/Corbis; p. 8 Joe McDonald/Visuals Unlimited; p. 9 Kennan Ward/Corbis; p. 10 Michael Durham/DRK Photo; p. 11 Robert Prickett/Corbis; p. 12 Frans Lanting/Minden Pictures; p. 13 Joe McDonald/DRK Photo; p. 14 P. Parks/NHPA; p. 15 Charles Melton/Visuals Unlimited; p. 16 Norbert Wu/DRK Photo; p. 17 Index Stock Imagery; p. 18 Dave B. Fleetham/Visuals Unlimited; p. 19 Corbis; p. 20 Philippe Moulu/Vandystadt/Photo Researchers, Inc.; p. 21 Courtesy Warner Brothers; p. 22 (row 1, L-R) Kennan Ward/Corbis, Michael Durham/DRK Photo; (row 2, L-R) Charles Melton/Visuals Unlimited, Courtesy Warner Brothers; p. 23 (row 1, L-R) Charles Melton/Visuals Unlimited, Joe McDonald/DRK Photo, Jane McAlonan/Visuals Unlimited; (row 2, L-R) Dave B. Fleetham/Visuals Unlimited, Frans Lanting/Minden Pictures, Robert Prickett/Corbis; (row 3, L-R) Norbert Wu/DRK Photo, Corbis, Courtesy Warner Brothers; (row 4, L-R) Norbert Wu/DRK Photo, Index Stock Imagery, Philippe Moulu/Vandystadt/Photo Researchers, Inc.; p. 24 (row 1, L-R) Michael Durham/DRK Photo, Charles Melton/Visuals Unlimited; (row 2) Kennan Ward/Corbis; (row 3) Courtesy Warner Brothers; back cover (L-R) Joe McDonald/Visuals Unlimited, Corbis

Cover photograph by Maslowski/Visuals Unlimited

Special thanks to our advisory panel for their help in the preparation of this book:

Alice Bethke, Library Consultant
Palo Alto, CA

Eileen Day, Preschool Teacher
Chicago, IL

Kathleen Gilbert,
Second Grade Teacher
Round Rock, TX

Sandra Gilbert,
Library Media Specialist
Fiest Elementary School
Houston, TX

Jan Gobeille,
Kindergarten Teacher
Garfield Elementary
Oakland, CA

Angela Leeper,
Educational Consultant
Wake Forest, NC

Some words are shown in bold, **like this.**
You can find them in the picture glossary on page 23.

Contents

What Is Flying?

Flying is a way of moving.

Living things that fly move through the air.

They start out on the ground or in the water.

They push themselves up with their wings.

How Do Living and Nonliving Things Fly?

wing

Living things that fly have wings.

They move their wings to keep flying.

wing

Nonliving things that fly have wings, too.

But these wings do not move.

Can Birds Fly?

feathers

Birds' wings are covered with feathers.

The feathers help some birds fly.

Ostriches have feathers on their wings, too.

But ostriches are birds that are too heavy to fly.

Can Bugs Fly?

Bees are bugs with wings.

Bees can fly.

Springtails are bugs that cannot fly.

But they can jump and crawl through dirt.

Can Small Animals Fly?

This bat is called a **fruit bat.**

It can fly.

Flying squirrels are small animals that cannot fly.

Instead, they glide from tree to tree.

How Many Wings Do Things Need?

Some things can fly with two wings.

Mosquitoes only have two wings.

Some things need more wings to fly.

Dragonflies have four wings.

Can Fish Fly?

fin

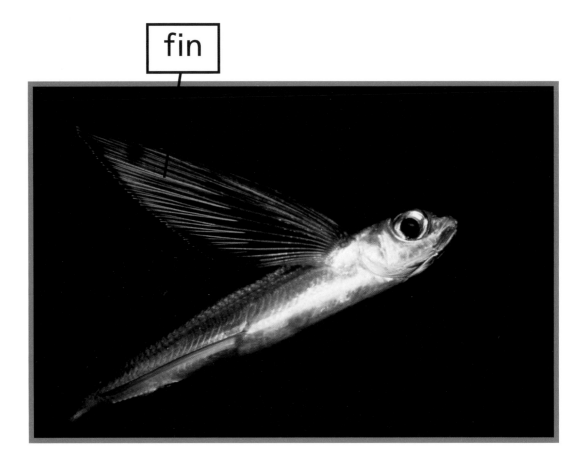

A **flying fish** has big **fins** that look like wings.

A flying fish can jump high, but it cannot fly.

fin

A **sailfish** has a big fin on top of its body.

It jumps out of the water, but it cannot fly.

Can Machines Fly?

engine

Airplanes can fly.

Jet **engines** push airplanes through the sky.

propellers

Helicopters can fly.

Spinning **propellers** lift them
into the sky.

Can People Fly?

People cannot fly by themselves.

This woman is flying in an **ultralight** plane.

Superheroes fly in movies.

But they are just pretending.

Quiz

Which of these things can fly?

Can you find them in the book?

Picture Glossary

dragonfly
page 15

flying squirrel
page 13

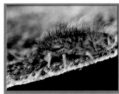

springtail
page 11

engine
page 18

fruit bat
page 12

superhero
page 21

fin
pages 16, 17

propeller
page 19

ultralight
page 20

flying fish
page 16

sailfish
page 17

23

Note to Parents and Teachers

Reading for information is an important part of a child's literacy development. Learning begins with a question about something. Help children think of themselves as investigators and researchers by encouraging their questions about the world around them. Each chapter in this book begins with a question that helps categorize the types of things that fly. Read each question together. Look at the pictures. Can children think of other flying things in each category? Discuss where you might find the answers. Assist children in using the picture glossary and the index to practice new vocabulary and research skills.

Index

Answers to quiz on page 22

Bees and dragonflies can fly.

Ostriches cannot fly.

People cannot fly by themselves.